Dogs on the Farm

by Mari C. Schuh

Welsh Corgi

Consulting Editor: Gail Saunders-Smith, Ph.D.

Consultant: Cary J. Trexler, Ph.D., Assistant Professor
Department of Agricultural Education and Studies
Iowa State University

Pebble Books

an imprint of Capstone Press
Mankato, Minnesota

Pebble Books are published by Capstone Press
151 Good Counsel Drive, P.O. Box 669, Mankato, Minnesota 56002
www.capstonepress.com

2 3 4 5 6 07 06 05 04 03 02

Library of Congress Cataloging-in-Publication Data
Schuh, Mari C., 1975–
    Dogs on the farm / by Mari C. Schuh.
    p. cm.—(On the farm)
    Includes bibliographical references (p. 23) and index.
    Summary: Simple text and photographs introduce dogs and their lives on
the farm.
    ISBN-13: 978-0-7368-1187-3 (hardcover)
    ISBN-10: 0-7368-1187-7 (hardcover)
    ISBN-13: 978-0-7368-9378-7 (softcover pbk.)
    ISBN-10: 0-7368-9378-4 (softcover pbk.)
    1. Dogs—Juvenile literature. [1. Dogs. 2. Farm life.] I. Title. II. Series.
SF426.5 .S34 2002
636.7—dc21   2001003314

Note to Parents and Teachers

The On the Farm series supports national science standards related
to life science. This book describes and illustrates dogs and their
lives on the farm. The photographs support early readers in
understanding the text. The repetition of words and phrases helps
early readers learn new words. This book also introduces early
readers to subject-specific vocabulary words, which are defined in
the Words to Know section. Early readers may need assistance to
read some words and to use the Table of Contents, Words to
Know, Read More, Internet Sites, and Index/Word List sections
of the book.

Table of Contents

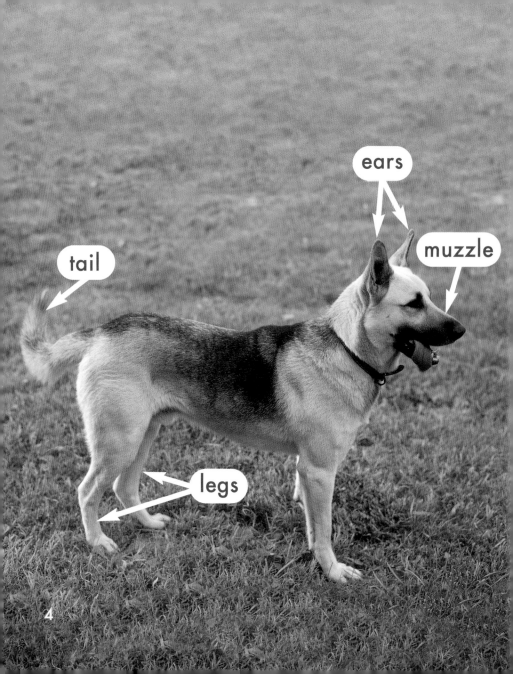

ears

muzzle

tail

legs

Some dogs live and work on farms and ranches.

German Shepherd

Many dogs live
outdoors. Some
dogs live in barns
or in homes.

Great Pyrenees

Farmers feed dogs
dog food and a lot
of water.

Border Collie

Some farmers
train dogs to work.

Welsh Corgi

Some dogs protect livestock from predators. These dogs bark when livestock is in danger.

German Shepherd

Some dogs herd livestock. Herding dogs round up the livestock and keep them together.

Collie

Farm dogs run
and play in fields.

Old English Sheepdog

Dogs do not sweat. They pant to stay cool.

Border Collie

Dogs wag their tails.

Border Collie

Words to Know

bark—to make a sound like a dog; dogs sometimes bark when they sense danger.

danger—a situation that is not safe

guard—to carefully watch an animal so that it does not get hurt or attacked

herd—to make animals move together as a group; some farm dogs herd groups of sheep and cattle.

livestock—animals raised on a farm or ranch; horses, sheep, and cows are livestock.

predator—an animal that hunts other animals for food; some farm dogs protect sheep from predators such as coyotes; dogs sometimes bite predators.

protect—to keep something from harm, attack, or injury

ranch—a large farm for cattle, sheep, or horses

Read More

Luke, Melinda. *Helping Paws: Dogs That Serve.* Hello Reader! New York: Scholastic, 2001.

McGinty, Alice B. *Sheepherding Dogs: Rounding up the Herd.* Dogs Helping People. New York: PowerKids Press, 1999.

Shahan, Sherry. *Working Dogs.* Planet Reader. Mahwah, N.J.: Troll Communications, 1999.

Internet Sites

Track down many sites about dogs. Visit the FactHound at *http://www.facthound.com*

IT IS EASY! IT IS FUN!

1) Go to *http://www.facthound.com*

2) Type in: 0736811877

3) Click on "FETCH IT" and FactHound will find several links hand-picked by our editors.

Relax and let our pal FactHound do the research for you!

Index/Word List

Word Count: 85
Early-Intervention Level: 11

Credits

Heather Kindseth, cover designer; Heidi Meyer, production designer; Kimberly Danger and Deirdre Barton, photo researchers

Capstone Press/Gary Sundermeyer, cover, 8, 18, 20; Jim Foell, 12
Kent & Donna Dannen, 6, 14
Mark Raycroft, 16
Norvia Behling, 1, 10
Unicorn Stock Photos/Charles E. Schmidt, 4